# BRITISH WARSHIPS 1975

by

J. W. GOSS

Published by

MARINART LTD.

DISTRIBUTED IN CANADA BY:
NEVASA PUBLICATIONS LTD.
P.O. BOX 86715
NORTH VANCOUVER, B.C.
V7L 4L2

# INTRODUCTION

Here at last is an inexpensive book which I hope will fill a gap that has been vacant for far too long

As a student of Naval affairs for many years and a keen naval photographer, I have often wished that there was a book available that I could pop into my pocket or keep handy on my desk containing the basic details of ships of the Royal Navy in an easy to find layout. I know that there is a wealth of naval reference books already available but I find these in general are aimed at the serious student who already knows what he is looking for, while the person with just a general interest or the young beginner finds himself floundering in a mass of detail. I am aiming for the younger enthusiasts and the person with just a general interest who does not wish to buy the more expensive books, though I am sure that the serious student will also find this book extremely useful as a quick and handy reference. Mainly I want to interest the new recruit to the field of naval study with the hope that my little book with its untraditional but easy to understand layout will whet his appetite and bring him into the ever growing field of naval enthusiasts.

With this in mind I thought of a system that will answer the need. I decided that the main theme of the book would be A. Easy to find and B. Basic details. For A I use the most noticeable thing on a warship. This is the large letter and number painted on the ship's side and on the stern. The correct naval term for these letters and numbers are Pennant Numbers. This is the ship's official number and when entering or leaving harbour, flags or pennants are flown from the yard denoting the ship's letter and number. So the first part of the book contains a list of these numbers in alphabetical and numerical order. If you spot a ship bearing the number F38, turn to the list and alphabetically the letter F then numerically the number 38 after which will appear the ship's name ARETHUSA and a page number to turn to for the details.

I am certain that ship spotters and photographers will find this list extremely useful as it is possible to identify a ship quickly, without searching through the whole book. Once found, a quick reference can be made to the appropriate page for details. In the case of photographers where there is not always time or convenience to refer immediately, the name can be noted, and reference made as time permits.

Just to make things interesting although all naval vessels have pennant numbers, not all of them paint them up. Submarines make spotting difficult although sometimes when entering or leaving harbour they do have a small plate bearing their name, fitted on the side of the fin, it is usually quite small and one needs to be fairly close or have binoculars to be able to read it.

Other vessels without numbers are the numerous small craft and
tenders to be seen in and around all naval ports. They are manned
by civilians employed by the Ministry of Defence and their ships
include tugs, tenders, salvage vessels, small cargo ships and tankers,
tank cleaning vessels, etc. Collectively they are known as PAS craft.
PAS standing for Port Auxiliary Service. They are however, readily
recognisable by their colour scheme of black hulls and buff upper-
works or black hulls and dark grey upper-works. While they all
carry their names in large readable letters at each side of the bow
and at the stern, some of the paddle tugs have their names at the
top of the paddle boxes or each side of the bridge. All the PAS
craft do a very important job of work and without them the navy
of fighting ships would be unable to operate. They are very interesting craft and have always been great favourites of mine.

All these vessels will be found in the Alphabetical list of names
which appears after the list of pennant numbers.


In the section dealing with basic details, will be found the ships
arranged by classes and types, with ship's number where applicable,
builders date of construction. Where dates appear thus — 1961-64
this denotes the ship was laid down in 1961 and completed in 1964.
Where only one date is given this denotes the completion date. Most
warships have a table of armaments which is correct to date. The
table is so laid out that one can add or delete weapons from one's
own observations so keeping the information up to date. The
measurement of each ship is given in tons, where two figures appear
the first is the standard Displacement and the second is full load.
The dimensions are in metres and are to the nearest centimetre.
First figure is length overall, then beam, then draught. Type of
machinery is shown with top speed. Differences in armament and
appearance in ships of the same class are shown in drawings and
tables, also mentioned in captions to photographs. No doubt many
of you will find items I have missed or not had space to mention.
If you do, I shall be very pleased as it means that the object of
this book, to whet your appetite and make you take notice, has
been achieved.

If by this book I am able to bring others into the world of
warships and Naval history I shall feel that my efforts have been
well rewarded.

The photographs are all by the author except for WHIRLWIND
from P. A. Vicary. The drawings are by Michael C. Easey. I acknow-
ledge reference to Janes Fighting Ships and Marine News and from
friends too numerous to mention who know me as a familiar figure
at Old Portsmouth with my cameras, and have helped me with their
observations.

James W. Goss<br>
Portsmouth 1975

3

| | | | | | | |
|---|---|---|---|---|---|---|
| F40 | Sirius | 28 | | F131 | Nubian | 36 |
| F41 | Volage | 86 | | F133 | Tartar | 36 |
| F42 | Phoebe | 28 | | F138 | Rapid | 86 |
| F43 | Torquay | 32 | | F187 | Whirlwind | 86 |
| F45 | Minerva | 28 | | F169 | Amazon | 26 |
| F47 | Danae | 28 | | F170 | Antelope | 26 |
| F48 | Dundas | 38 | | F171 | Active | 26 |
| F52 | Juno | 28 | | F172 | Ambuscade | 26 |
| F53 | Undaunted | 86 | | F173 | Arrow | 26 |
| F54 | Hardy | 38 | | F174 | Ardent | 26 |
| F56 | Argonaut | 28 | | F175 | Alacrity | 26 |
| F57 | Andromeda | 28 | | F176 | Avenger | 26 |
| F58 | Hermione | 28 | | | | |
| F59 | Chichester | 34 | | GHA01 | Invincible | 8 |
| F60 | Jupiter | 28 | | GHA02 | Indefatigable | 8 |
| F61 | Llandaff | 34 | | GHA03 | Inflexible | 8 |
| F63 | Scarborough | 32 | | | | |
| F65 | Tenby | 32 | | K07 | Lofoten | 8 |
| F69 | Bacchante | 28 | | K08 | Engadine | 8 |
| F70 | Apollo | 28 | | | | |
| F71 | Scylla | 28 | | L10 | Fearless | 13 |
| F72 | Ariadne | 28 | | L11 | Intrepid | 8 |
| F73 | Eastbourne | 32 | | L3004 | Sir Bedivere | 18 |
| F75 | Charybdis | 28 | | L3005 | Sir Galahad | 18 |
| F76 | Mermaid | 36 | | L3016 | Dieppe | 18 |
| F77 | Blackpool | 32 | | L3027 | Sir Geraint | 18 |
| F78 | Blackwood | 38 | | L3029 | Sir Lancelot | 18 |
| F84 | Exmouth | 38 | | L3036 | Sir Percivale | 18 |
| F85 | Keppel | 38 | | L3043 | Messina | 18 |
| F88 | Malcolm | 38 | | L3044 | Narvick | 18 |
| F94 | Palliser | 38 | | L3505 | Sir Tristram | 18 |
| F97 | Russell | 38 | | L3515 | Stalker | 18 |
| F99 | Lincoln | 34 | | L3532 | Zeebrugge | 18 |
| F101 | Yarmouth | 32 | | L4002 | Agheila | 18 |
| F103 | Lowestoft | 32 | | L4037 | Akyab | 18 |
| F104 | Dido | 28 | | L4041 | Abbeville | 18 |
| F106 | Brighton | 32 | | L4061 | Audemer | 18 |
| F107 | Rothesay | 32 | | L4062 | Aachen | 18 |
| F108 | Londonderry | 32 | | L4974 | Antwerp | 18 |
| F109 | Leander | 28 | | L4097 | Andalnes | 18 |
| F113 | Falmouth | 32 | | L4128 | Arrezzo | 18 |
| F114 | Ajax | 28 | | L4164 | Arrakan | 18 |
| F115 | Berwick | 32 | | | | |
| F117 | Ashanti | 36 | | M1103 | Kilmorey | 40 |
| F119 | Eskimo | 36 | | M1109 | Killiecrankie | 40 |
| F122 | Gurkha | 36 | | M1110 | Bildeston | 40 |
| F124 | Zulu | 36 | | M1112 | Boulston | 40 |
| F125 | Mohawk | 36 | | M1113 | Brereton | 40 |
| F126 | Plymouth | 32 | | M1114 | Brinton | 40 |
| F127 | Penelope | 28 | | M1115 | Bronington | 40 |
| F129 | Rhyl | 32 | | M1116 | Wilton | 40 |
| | | | | M1124 | St. David | 40 |
| | | | | M1125 | Cuxton | 40 |

| | | | | | |
|---|---|---|---|---|---|
| M1130 | Highburton | 40 | M2716 | Pagham | 44 |
| M1133 | Bossington | 40 | M2717 | Fordham | 44 |
| M1136 | Curzon | 40 | M2726 | Shipham | 44 |
| M1140 | Gavinton | 40 | M2733 | Thakeham | 44 |
| M1141 | Glasserton | 40 | M2735 | Tongham | 44 |
| M1145 | Dufton | 40 | M2781 | Portisham | 44 |
| M1146 | Venturer | 40 | M2783 | Odiham | 44 |
| M1147 | Hubberston | 40 | M2784 | Puttenham | 44 |
| M1150 | Invermoriston | 40 | M2785 | Birdham | 44 |
| M1151 | Investon | 40 | M2790 | Thatcham | 44 |
| M1153 | Kedleston | 40 | M2791 | Sandringham | 44 |
| M1154 | Kellington | 40 | M2793 | Thornham | 44 |
| M1157 | Kirkliston | 40 | N13 | Miner 111 | 54 |
| M1158 | Laleston | 40 | N21 | Abdiel | 54 |
| M1161 | Leverton | 41 | | | |
| M1164 | Maddiston | 41 | P190 | Laymoor | 76 |
| M1165 | Maxton | 41 | P191 | Layburn | 76 |
| M1166 | Nurton | 41 | P202 | Barfoot | 76 |
| M1167 | Clyde | 41 | P232 | Barmond | 76 |
| M1173 | Mersey | 41 | P260 | Kingfisher | 46 |
| M1175 | Quainton | 41 | P261 | Cygnet | 46 |
| M1180 | Shavington | 41 | P262 | Petrel | 46 |
| M1181 | Sheraton | 41 | P263 | Sandpiper | 46 |
| M1182 | Shoulton | 41 | P271 | Scimitar | 46 |
| M1187 | Upton | 41 | P274 | Cutlass | 46 |
| M1188 | Walkerton | 41 | P275 | Sabre | 46 |
| M1192 | Wilkeston | 41 | P276 | Tenacity | 46 |
| M1194 | Thames | 41 | P1007 | Beachampton | 46 |
| M1195 | Wotton | 41 | P1055 | Moncton | 46 |
| M1198 | Ashton | 41 | P1089 | Wasperton | 46 |
| M1199 | Belton | 41 | P1093 | Wolverton | 46 |
| M1200 | Soberton | 41 | P1096 | Yarnton | 46 |
| M1204 | Montrose | 41 | R08 | Bulwark | 8 |
| M1205 | Northumbria | 41 | R09 | Ark Royal | 8 |
| M1206 | Fiskerton | 41 | R12 | Hermes | 8 |
| M1208 | Lewiston | 41 | RPL01 | Avon | 84 |
| M1209 | Chawton | 41 | RPL02 | Bude | 84 |
| M1216 | Solent | 41 | RPL03 | Clyde | 84 |
| M2002 | Aveley | 43 | RPL04 | Dart | 84 |
| M2010 | Isis | 43 | RPL05 | Eden | 84 |
| M2603 | Arlingham | 43 | RPL06 | Forth | 84 |
| M2611 | Bottisham | 43 | RPL07 | Glen | 84 |
| M2614 | Bucklesham | 43 | RPL08 | Hamble | 84 |
| M2616 | Chelsham | 43 | RPL10 | Kennet | 84 |
| M2621 | Dittisham | 43 | RPL11 | Loddon | 84 |
| M2622 | Downham | 43 | RPL12 | Medway | 84 |
| M2624 | Elsingham | 43 | | | |
| M2626 | Everingham | 43 | WB03 | Bream | 84 |
| M2628 | Flintham | 43 | WB04 | Barbel | 84 |
| M2630 | Fritham | 43 | WB05 | Roach | 84 |
| M2635 | Haversham | 43 | WB06 | Perch | 84 |
| M2636 | Lasham | 44 | WB07 | Pike | 84 |

| | | | |
|---|---:|---|---:|
| Cairn | 71 | Derwentdale | 60 |
| Cachalot | 50 | Devonshire | 23 |
| Caldy | 76 | Dewdale | 60 |
| Caprice | 86 | Dexterous | 67 |
| Cardiff | 22 | Diamond | 86 |
| Cartmel | 80 | Dido | 28 |
| Cavalier | 86 | Dieppe | 18 |
| Cawsand | 80 | Director | 67 |
| Celia | 73 | Diomede | 28 |
| Charlotte | 73 | Dispenser | 76 |
| Charybdis | 28 | Dittisham | 43 |
| Chawton | 41 | Dolwen | 78 |
| Chelsham | 43 | Doris | 73 |
| Cherryleaf | 60 | Dornoch | 80 |
| Chichester | 34 | Dorothy | 73 |
| Christine | 73 | Downham | 43 |
| Churchill | 48 | Dreadnought | 48 |
| Cicala | 82 | Dufton | 40 |
| Claire | 73 | Duncan | 38 |
| Cleopatra | 28 | Dundas | 38 |
| Clovelly | 82 | Dunster | 80 |
| Clyde | 41 | | |
| Clyde RPL | 84 | Eastbourne | 32 |
| Cockchafer | 82 | Echo | 52 |
| Coll | 76 | Eddyfirth | 60 |
| Collie | 71 | Eden | 84 |
| Confiance | 67 | Edith | 73 |
| Confident | 67 | Egeria | 52 |
| Conqueror | 48 | Elkhound | 71 |
| Corgi | 71 | Elkstone | 80 |
| Courageous | 48 | Elsing | 80 |
| Coventry | 22 | Elsingham | 43 |
| Criccieth | 80 | Eminent | 75 |
| Cricket | 82 | Empire Ace | 75 |
| Cricklade | 80 | Empire Demon | 75 |
| Cromarty | 80 | Empire Fred | 75 |
| Crystal | 54 | Empire Netta | 75 |
| Curzon | 40 | Empire Rosa | 75 |
| Cutlass | 46 | Endurance | 52 |
| Cuxton | 40 | Engadine | 8 |
| Cyclone | 67 | Enterprise | 52 |
| Cygnet | 46 | Epworth | 80 |
| | | Eskimo | 36 |
| Daisy | 73 | Ettrick | 81 |
| Dalmatian | 71 | Euryalus | 28 |
| Danae | 28 | Everingham | 43 |
| Daphne | 73 | Exmouth | 38 |
| Dart | 84 | | |
| Datchet | 80 | Faithful | 67 |
| Deerhound | 71 | Falmouth | 32 |
| Defiance | 54 | Favourite | 67 |
| Denmead | 80 | Fawn | 52 |

| Kennet | 84 |
| Kent | 23 |
| Keppel | 38 |
| Kinbrace | 76 |
| Kingarth | 76 |
| Kinloss | 76 |
| Kinterbury | 62 |
| Kirkliston | 40 |
| Kilmorey | 40 |
| Killiecrankie | 40 |
| Kingfisher | 46 |
| Kitty | 73 |
| | |
| L 700—11 | 19 |
| L 3507—8 | 19 |
| LCM | 19 |
| LCVP | 20 |
| Labrador | 71 |
| Ladybird | 82 |
| Laleston | 40 |
| Lamlash | 81 |
| Lasham | 44 |
| Layburn | 76 |
| Laymoor | 76 |
| Leander | 28 |
| Lechlade | 81 |
| Leopard | 34 |
| Lesley | 73 |
| Leverton | 41 |
| Lewiston | 41 |
| Lilah | 73 |
| Lilian | 73 |
| Lincoln | 34 |
| Llandaff | 34 |
| Llandovery | 81 |
| Loddon | 84 |
| Lofoten | 8 |
| London | 23 |
| Londonderry | 32 |
| Lowestoft | 32 |
| Loyal Chancellor | 81 |
| Loyal Factor | 82 |
| Loyal Governor | 82 |
| Loyal Moderator | 82 |
| Loyal Proctor | 82 |
| Lundy | 76 |
| Lyness | 62 |
| Lynx | 34 |
| | |
| Maddiston | 41 |
| Maidstone | 54 |
| Malcolm | 38 |
| Mandarin | 76 |
| Martin | 84 |
| Mary | 73 |
| Mastiff | 71 |
| Matapan | 54 |
| Maxton | 41 |
| May | 73 |
| Medway | 84 |
| Mermaid | 36 |
| Mersey | 41 |
| Messina | 18 |
| Miner 111 | 54 |
| Minerva | 28 |
| Mohawk | 36 |
| Moncton | 46 |
| Montrose | 41 |
| Mull | 84 |
| Myrtle | 73 |
| | |
| NST | 20 |
| Naiad | 28 |
| Nancy | 73 |
| Narvick | 18 |
| Narwhal | 50 |
| Newman Bloggs | 84 |
| Newcastle | 22 |
| Nimble | 67 |
| Norfolk | 23 |
| Norah | 73 |
| Northumbria | 41 |
| Nubian | 36 |
| Nurton | 41 |
| | |
| Oberon | 50 |
| Ocelot | 50 |
| Odiham | 44 |
| Odin | 50 |
| Oilbird | 60 |
| Oilfield | 60 |
| Oilman | 60 |
| Oilpress | 60 |
| Oilstone | 60 |
| Oilwell | 60 |
| Oliver Twist | 84 |
| Olmeda | 58 |
| Olna | 58 |
| Olwen | 58 |
| Olympus | 50 |
| Onslaught | 50 |
| Onyx | 50 |
| Opossum | 50 |
| Oracle | 50 |

| | | | |
|---|---|---|---|
| Opportune | 50 | Sabre | 46 |
| Orangeleaf | 60 | Salisbury | 34 |
| Orpheus | 50 | Saluki | 71 |
| Osiris | 50 | Salvalour | 78 |
| Otter | 50 | Salveda | 78 |
| Otus | 50 | Samson | 67 |
| | | Sandpiper | 46 |
| Pagham | 44 | Sandringham | 44 |
| Palliser | 38 | Sarpeta | 54 |
| Pearleaf | 60 | Scarab | 82 |
| Perch | 84 | Scarborough | 32 |
| Penelope | 28 | Sceptre | 48 |
| Petrel | 46 | Scimitar | 46 |
| Phoebe | 28 | Scylla | 28 |
| Pike | 84 | Sea Salvour | 78 |
| Pintail | 76 | Seagiant | 67 |
| Plymouth | 32 | Sealion | 50 |
| Pochard | 76 | Sealyham | 71 |
| Pointer | 71 | Security | 75 |
| Porpoise | 50 | Setter | 71 |
| Porqual | 50 | Shavington | 41 |
| Portisham | 44 | Sheepdog | 71 |
| Prompt | 75 | Sheffield | 22 |
| Puma | 34 | Sheraton | 41 |
| Puttenham | 44 | Shipham | 44 |
| | | Shoulton | 41 |
| Quainton | 41 | Sir Bedivere | 18 |
| | | Sir Galahad | 18 |
| RNAL 54 | 78 | Sir Geraint | 18 |
| Rame Head | 62 | Sir Lancelot | 18 |
| Rapid | 86 | Sir Percivale | 18 |
| Reclaim | 54 | Sir Tristram | 18 |
| Regent | 62 | Sirius | 28 |
| Reliant | 62 | Skomer | 76 |
| Renown | 48 | Skua | 84 |
| Repulse | 48 | Smike | 84 |
| Resolve | 75 | Soberton | 41 |
| Resolution | 48 | Solent | 41 |
| Resource | 62 | Sovereign | 48 |
| Resurgent | 62 | Spabrook | 66 |
| Retainer | 62 | Spaburn | 66 |
| Reward | 67 | Spalake | 66 |
| Revenge | 48 | Spapool | 66 |
| Rhyl | 32 | Spaniel | 76 |
| Roach | 84 | Spartan | 48 |
| Robert Middleton | 62 | St David | 40 |
| Robust | 67 | St Margarets | 78 |
| Rollicker | 67 | Stalker | 18 |
| Rothesay | 32 | Steady | 54 |
| Roysterer | 67 | Stromness | 62 |
| Russell | 38 | Superb | 48 |

# AIR SUPPORT SHIPS

| Number | Name | Builder | Date of Bldg |
|---|---|---|---|
| R08 | BULWARK | Har.Wolff | 1945—54 |
| R12 | HERMES | Vickers | 1944—59 |
| R09 | ARK ROYAL | Cam.Laird | 1943—55 |
| GHA01 | INVINCIBLE | Vickers | 1973 |
| GHA02 | INDEFATIGABLE | | |
| GHA03 | INFLEXIBLE | | |
| C20 | TIGER | Brown | 1941—59 |
| C99 | BLAKE | Fairfield | 1942—61 |
| L10 | FEARLESS | Har.Wolff | 1962—65 |
| L11 | INTREPID | Brown | 1962—67 |
| K08 | ENGADINE | Robb | 1965—67 |
| K07 | LOFOTEN | Blyth | 1946 |

BULWARK — Wessex helicopters on deck. LCVP alongside

# R08 BULWARK R12 HERMES

Both these ships were formerly fixed wing aircraft carriers and are now Helicopter carriers. BULWARK was converted in 1960 and HERMES in 1971—73. Able to operate anti-sub and assault helicopters they will eventually be replaced by the INVINCIBLE class. BULWARK will be laid up within next 12 months.

M      R08 23,000/27,700     (R12 23,900/28,700)
D      R08 224.9 x 27.4 x 8.5    (R12 226.9 x 27.4 x 8.5)
Mch    Both st. 76,000 shp. = 28k
C      2,000 plus including aircrew and Commandos

## ARK ROYAL

Last fixed wing carrier in service, no more ships of this type are planned. Airpower at sea will in future be carried by ship like INVINCIBLE.

M      43,060/50,786
D      275.6 x 34.4 x 11
Mch    ST 152,000 shp. = 31.5k
C      2740 including aircrew

## INVINCIBLE

Three of this type planned. They will be capable of operating helicopters and VTO fixed wing aircraft. The following details are estimated.

M      19,000/20,000
D      198.1 x 25.6 x 7.3
Mch    GT30k
C      750

# C20 TIGER C99 BLAKE

These two six inch gun cruisers of WW11 design are of a class of 5. Two were cancelled and the other scrapped. Not completed at wars end they were laid up for 8 years then commissioned as cruisers. BLAKE was converted in 1965—69 and TIGER 1969—73. Present role Command ship/helicopter carrier.

```
M      9,500/12,080
D      172.8 x 64 x 7
Mch    ST 80,000 shp. 31.5k
C      885
```

# L10 FEARLESS L11 INTREPID

Very useful ships with multicapabilities, able to operate VTO fixed wing and helicopters. Can be used as Command ships, assault ships for air or sea landings, landing craft being stowed under the flight deck and launched by opening stern gate and flooding down enabling them to float out.

```
Displ   10,550/12,500 full l . 19,500 flooded down
D.      158.5 x  24.4 x 8.4
Mch     ST 22,000 shp. 21k
C       667 including aircrew and army
```

# K08 ENGADINE

Built for training helicopter crews but has a role as a helicopter transport or off shore base ship.

```
M      8,000/9,000
D      129 x 17 x 6
Mch    Dsl 5,500 bhp = 16k
C      188 (max)
```

# K07 LOFOTEN

Former landing ship modified to operate helicopters. in 1964. At present laid up.

```
M      2,140/4,820
D      104 x 16 x 2.5
Mch    TE 5,500 ihp =12½k
C      110
```

|        | 6" | 3" | 40mm | RP | SC | Aircraft | SD | EX |
|--------|----|----|------|----|----|----------|----|----|
| R08    |    |    | 8    | 2  |    | 22       |    |    |
| R12    |    |    |      | 1  | 4  | 20       |    |    |
| R09    |    |    |      | 2  | 4  | 38       |    |    |
| R      |    |    |      |    |    |          |    |    |
| C20    | 2  | 2  |      | 2  | 2  | 4        |    |    |
| C99    | 2  | 2  |      | 2  | 2  | 4        |    |    |
| L10    |    |    | 2    | 2  | 4  | 6        |    |    |
| L11    |    |    | 2    | 2  | 4  | 6        |    |    |
| K08    |    |    |      |    |    | 6        |    |    |
| K07    |    |    | 2    |    |    | 6        |    |    |
| GHA01  |    |    |      |    |    |          | 2  | 2  |
| GHA02  |    |    |      |    |    |          | 2  | 2  |
| GHA03  |    |    |      |    |    |          | 2  | 2  |

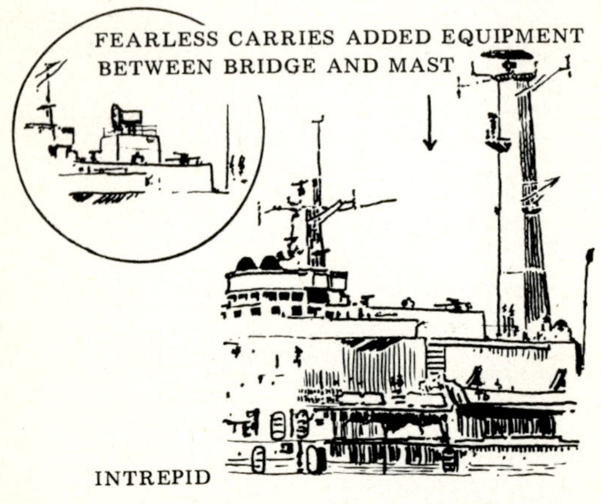

TIGER — Taller funnel than BLAKE, last 6in. gun ship in Navy

FEARLESS — Staggered funnels, tall tower mast
Carries 'Skynet' communications system

ENGADINE — Mercantile appearance. Mast on f'c'sle

# AMPHIBIOUS CRAFT

| Number | Name | Builder | Date of Building |
|---|---|---|---|
| L3004 | SIR BEDIVERE | Hawthorn | 1965—67 |
| L3005 | SIR GALAHAD | Stephen | 1965—66 |
| L3027 | SIR GERAINT | Stephen | 1965—67 |
| L3029 | SIR LANCELOT | Fairfield | 1962—64 |
| L3036 | SIR PERCIVALE | Hawthorn | 1966—68 |
| L3505 | SIR TRISTRAM | Hawthorn | 1966—67 |
| L3016 | DIEPPE | Hawthorn | 1945 |
| L3044 | NARVICK | Vickers | 1946 |
| L3043 | MESSINA | Scotts | 1945 |
| L3515 | STALKER | Yarrow | 1945 |
| L3532 | ZEEBRUGGE | Sorel | 1945 |
| L4002 | AGHEILA | | 1945—47 |
| L4037 | AKYAB | | 1945—47 |
| L4041 | ABBEVILLE | | 1945—47 |
| L4061 | AUDEMER | | 1945—47 |
| L4062 | AACHEN | | 1945—47 |
| L4074 | ANTWERP | | 1945—47 |
| L4097 | ANDALNES | | 1945—47 |
| L4128 | ARREZZO | | 1945—47 |
| L4164 | ARAKAN | | 1945—47 |

## SIR BEDIVERE Class

Dual purpose transports and landing ships at present manned by RFA. Capable of bow and stern loading and carry pontoons to provide a 240' causeway from ship to shore. All are able to operate helicopters. All types of military cargo from tanks to mobile cranes can be carried. If required could carry as cargo up to 20 helicopters.

M     3270/5674 (L3039 3370/5550)
D     124 x 18 x 3.5
Mch     Dsl 8460 bhp = 17k (L3059 8250 bhp = 17k)
C     69 (plus 400 troops)

## DIEPPE Class

All WW11 type LST 3s. As landing ships they could carry up to 29 vehicles depending on type and 168 troops. Post war they were adapted for other roles, L3044, L3515 as submarine support ships, see Ko7 helicopter support ship. All are now laid up and are used as store and accommodation ships.

M     2140/4820 F.1. (L3043 2255/4980 fl.)
D     105 x 16 x 3
Mch     TE. 5500 ihp = 13k
C     100

## AGHEILA Class

All WW11 type LCT 8. Manned by the Army. Can carry up to 8 tanks plus 42 troops.

M     657/900 f.l.
D     70 x 11 x 1.5
Mch     Dsl 2800 bhp = 12k
C     36

## LCM 9

Fourteen of this type were built, two prototypes L3507—8 and twelve production L700—11. All were completed 1966—67. Four are carried by FEARLESS and INTREPID.

M     75/176 f.l.
D     25.5 x 6 x 1.5
Mch     Dsl 550 bhp = 10k
C     8

# LCVP

About fifty of this type were built between 1956—66.
About fifteen to twenty remain in service.  They are carried
by assault ships and helicopter carriers.

```
M      11½/16½ f.l.
D.     13 x 3 x 0.5
Mch    Dsl  130 bhp 10k
C      4 plus 25 troops
```

# NST

Tenders for transporting men and cargo, carried aboard
Replenishment and store ships.

```
M
D
Mch    Dsl
C      3
```

MESSINA — Typical WWII landing ship. Note heavy davits
for hoisting out assault craft

ANDALSNES — Army manned. Bow doors

L706 — Note ramp

NST 6554 — Wooden construction
Twin screw vessel for ship to ship stores transfer

# MISSILE DESTROYERS

| Number | Name | Builder | Date of Building |
|--------|------|---------|------------------|
| D80 | SHEFFIELD | Vickers | 1970—74 |
| D86 | BIRMINGHAM | C. Laird | 1972— |
| D87 | NEWCASTLE | S. Hunter | 1973— |
| D88 | GLASGOW | S. Hunter | 1973— |
| D108 | CARDIFF | Vickers | 1972— |
| D118 | COVENTRY | Laird | 1972— |

SHEFFIELD — Two Radar Domes

# Type 42 SHEFFIELD Class

New type of guided missile destroyer with surface to air Sea Dart missile system. All will carry one Lynx helicopter.

M      3250/3600 f.l.
D      125 x 14.3 x
Mch   GT 50000 shp = 30k plus
C      280

| D | 4.5 | 20mm | RP | SD |
|---|---|---|---|---|
| D80 | 1 | 2 | 2 | 1 |
| D86 | 1 | 2 | | 1 |
| D87 | 1 | 2 | | 1 |
| D88 | 1 | 2 | | 1 |
| D108 | 1 | 2 | | 1 |
| D118 | 1 | 2 | | 1 |

| Number | Name | Builder | Date of Building |
|---|---|---|---|
| D02 | DEVONSHIRE | C. Laird | 1959—62 |
| D06 | HAMPSHIRE | L. Brown | 1959—63 |
| D12 | KENT | Har. Wolff | 1960—63 |
| D16 | LONDON | S. Hunter | 1961—63 |
| D18 | ANTRIM | Fairfield | 1966—70 |
| D19 | GLAMORGAN | Vickers | 1962—66 |
| D20 | FIFE | Fairfield | 1962—66 |
| D21 | NORFOLK | S. Hunter | 1966—70 |
| D23 | BRISTOL | S. Hunter | 1967—72 |

# County Class

This class were built to provide anti-aircraft cover for carrier task groups and as such have a powerful A/A capability combined with a long range and good sea keeping. Very handsome ships with nice clean lines all of them carry a helicopter. Four of them have recently been refitted and armed with exocet surface-to-surface missile launcher. HAMPSHIRE will be put on disposal list within the next 12 months.

```
M      5650/6750 f.l.
D      158.7 x 16.5 x 6.1
Mch    GT and ST 60000 shp = 32.5k
C      471
```

# Type 82 BRISTOL

Intended as a class of four but three were cancelled. Largest destroyer ever built for Royal Navy, BRISTOL has the most up-to-date electronic data control system for her weapon systems. She is capable of engaging submarine, air and surface targets.

```
M      5650/6750 f.l.
D      154.5 x 16.8 x 6.9
Mch    GT and ST 74600 shp = 30k. plus
C      433
```

|      | 4.5 | 20mm | IK | EX | SC | SS | SD | RP | L |
|------|-----|------|----|----|----|----|----|----|---|
| D02  | 4   | 2    |    |    | 2  | 1  |    | 2  |   |
| D06  | 4   | 2    |    |    | 2  | 1  |    | 2  |   |
| D12  | 4   | 2    |    |    | 2  | 1  |    | 2  |   |
| D16  | 4   | 2    |    |    | 2  | 1  |    | 2  |   |
| D18  | 2   | 2    |    | 2  | 2  | 1  |    | 2  |   |
| D19  | 2   | 2    |    | 2  | 2  | 1  |    | 2  |   |
| D20  | 2   | 2    |    | 2  | 2  | 1  |    | 2  |   |
| D21  | 2   | 2    |    | 2  | 2  | 1  |    | 2  |   |
| D23  | 1   |      | 1  |    |    |    | 1  |    | 1 |

GLAMORGAN — With 'Exocet' in place of 'B' gun

KENT — With 'B' gun

BRISTOL — Three funnels, tall mainmast

# MISSILE FRIGATES

| Number | Name | Builder | Date of Building |
|---|---|---|---|
| F | BATTLEAXE | | |
| F | BROADSWORD | Yarrow | 1975 |

## Type 22

New class of frigate to replace LEANDER class. Will be armed with Exocet and Sea Wolf missiles and carry Lynx helicopter.

M   3000 estimated
D
Mch  GT 30k

| Number | Name | Builder | Date of Building |
|---|---|---|---|
| F169 | AMAZON | Vosper | 1969—74 |
| F170 | ANTELOPE | Vosper | 1971—75 |
| F171 | ACTIVE | Vosper | 1971— |
| F172 | AMBUSCADE | Yarrow | 1971— |
| F173 | ARROW | Yarrow | 1972— |
| F174 | ARDENT | Yarrow | 1973— |
| F175 | ALACRITY | Yarrow | |
| F176 | AVENGER | Yarrow | |

Type 22 Frigate to be constructed by Yarrows
following the complete Leander Class

# Type 21 AMAZON Class

Patrol frigate designed for the navy by Vosper and Yarrow. The first warship to be designed for the Royal Navy by a commercial firm for some years. The result is a vessel of rakish yet very seaworthy design and the most handsome appearance of any class of warship built post-war. All will carry one Lynx helicopter.

| | | |
|---|---|---|
| M | 2500 f.l. |
| D | 117 x 12.7 x 3.7 |
| Mch | GT 50000 shp 35k plus |
| C | 170 |

| | 4.5 | 20mm | SC | RP |
|---|---|---|---|---|
| F169 | 1 | 2 | 1 | 2 |
| F170 | 1 | 2 | 1 | 2 |
| F171 | | | | |
| F172 | | | | |
| F173 | | | | |
| F174 | | | | |
| F175 | | | | |
| F176 | | | | |

AMAZON — Squat funnel

# CONVENTIONAL FRIGATES

| Number | Name | Builders | Date of Building | Grp | Nav. Radar |
|---|---|---|---|---|---|
| F10 | AURORA | J. Brown | 1961—1964 | 1st | F |
| F12 | ACHILLES | Yarrow | 1967—70 | 3rd | C |
| F15 | EURYALUS | Scotts | 1961—64 | 1st | F |
| F16 | DIOMEDE | Yarrow | 1968—71 | 3rd | C |
| F18 | GALATEA | S. Hunter | 1961—64 | 1st | F |
| F28 | CLEOPATRA | HMD Dev. | 1963—66 | 1st | |
| F38 | ARETHUSA | Whites | 1962—65 | 1st | F |
| F39 | NAIAD | Yarrow | 1962—65 | 1st | F |
| F40 | SIRIUS | HMD Ports | 1963—66 | 2nd | C |
| F42 | PHOEBE | Stephen | 1963—66 | 2nd | F |
| F45 | MINERVA | Vick.Arm. | 1963—66 | 2nd | C |
| F47 | DANAE | HMD Dev. | 1964—67 | 2nd | F |
| F52 | JUNO | Thorny | 1964—67 | 2nd | F |
| F56 | ARGONAUT | Hawthorn | 1964—67 | 2nd | C |
| F57 | ANDROMEDA | HMD Ports | 1966—68 | 3rd | C |
| F58 | HERMIONE | Stephen | 1965—69 | 3rd | C |
| 5F60 | JUPITER | Yarrow | 1966—69 | 3rd | C |
| F69 | BACCHANTE | Vickers | 1966—69 | 3rd | C |
| F70 | APOLLO | Yarrow | 1969—72 | 3rd | C |
| F71 | SCYLLA | HMD Dev. | 1968—70 | 3rd | C |
| F72 | ARIADNE | Yarrow | 1969—72 | 3rd | C |
| F75 | CHARYBDIS | Har.Wolff | 1967—69 | 3rd | C |
| F104 | DIDO | Yarrow | 1959—63 | 1st | F |
| F109 | LEANDER | Har.Wolff | 1959—63 | 1st | C |
| F114 | AJAX | Laird | 1959—63 | 1st | C |
| F127 | PENELOPE | Vick.Arm. | 1961—63 | 1st | F |

Nav Radar F  =  Facing forward  
Nav Radar C  =  Canted to one side

# 26 LEANDER Class

Largest class of major warship built for the Royal Navy since WWII. They are a follow on from the Whitby class, F104, 109 and 114 were to have been Whitbys. They have proved very successful in service and ships of the same basic design have been built for the Dutch, New Zealand and Chilean Navies. Four are under construction for the Indian Navy. They were built in three groups, ships of the third group having a broader beam. Some of the earlier ships are now ten years old but their large hulls have enabled them to be refitted with modern weapons and all of the class are to be fitted with Exocet or Ikara which will bring them right up-to-date. All carry one Wasp helicopter.

| | |
|---|---|
| M | 2450/2860 |
| | 3rd group 2500/2962 |
| D | 113.4 x 12.5 x 5.5 |
| Mch | ST 30000 shp 30k |
| C | 263 |

| No. | 4.5 | SW | IK | EX | 20 mm | 3" RP | 40 mm | SC | VDS | Lim | Fun Rig |
|---|---|---|---|---|---|---|---|---|---|---|---|
| F10 | 2 | | P | O | | | 2 | | Y | 1 | |
| F12 | 2 | | | P | 2 | 2 | | 1 | N | 1 | |
| F15 | 2 | | P | | | 2 | 2 | | N | 1 | |
| F16 | 2 | | | P | 2 | 2 | | 1 | N | 1 | |
| F18 | 0 | | 1 | | | 2 | 2 | 2 | Y | 1 | Y |
| F28 | 2 | | | P | 2 | 2 | | 1 | Y | 1 | |
| F38 | 2 | | P | | 2 | 2 | | 1 | Y | 1 | |
| F39 | 2 | | P | | 2 | 2 | | 1 | Y | 1 | |
| F40 | 2 | | | P | 2 | 2 | | 1 | N | 1 | |
| F42 | 2 | | | P | 2 | 2 | | 1 | N | 1 | |
| F45 | 2 | | | P | 2 | 2 | | 1 | N | 1 | |
| F47 | 2 | | | P | 2 | | | 1 | N | 1 | |
| F52 | 2 | | | P | 2 | 2 | | 1 | N | 1 | |

|  |  |  |  |  |  |  |  |  |  |  |
| --- | --- | --- | --- | --- | --- | --- | --- | --- | --- | --- |
| F56 | 2 |  | P | 2 | 2 |  | 1 | N | 1 |  |
| F57 | 2 |  | P | 2 | 2 |  | 1 | N | 1 |  |
| F58 | 2 |  | P | 2 | 2 |  | 1 | Y | 1 |  |
| F60 | 2 |  | P | 2 | 2 |  | 1 | Y | 1 |  |
| F69 | 2 |  | P | 2 | 2 |  | 1 | Y | 1 |  |
| F70 | 2 |  | P | 2 | 2 |  | 1 | N | 1 |  |
| F71 | 2 |  | P | 2 | 2 |  | 1 | N | 1 |  |
| F72 | 2 |  | P | 2 | 2 |  | 1 | N | 1 |  |
| F75 | 2 |  | P | 2 | 2 |  | 1 | Y | 1 |  |
| F104 | 2 |  | P |  | 2 | 2 |  | Y | 1 |  |
| F109 |  |  | 1 |  | 2 | 2 | 2 | Y | 1 | Y |
| F114 |  |  | 1 |  | 2 | 2 | 2 | Y | 1 | Y |
| F127 |  | 1 | P |  |  |  |  | Y |  |  |

JUNO — Rocket projectors and 'Seacat'

**BACCHANTE — Cut-away stern housing VDS**

**ARIADNE — Clear decks fore and aft. All
supersructure amidships**

**JUNO — No VDS**

| Number | Name | Builders | Date of Building | Class |
|---|---|---|---|---|
| F36 | WHITBY | Laird | 1952—56 | W |
| F43 | TORQUAY | Har.Wolff | 1953—56 | W |
| F63 | SCARBOROUGH | Vick.Arm. | 1953—57 | W |
| F65 | TENBY | Laird | 1953—57 | W |
| F73 | EASTBOURNE | Vick.Arm. | 1955—58 | W |
| F77 | BLACKPOOL | Har.Wolff | 1954—58 | W |
| F101 | YARMOUTH | J.Brown | 1957—60 | R |
| F103 | LOWESTOFT | Stephen | 1958—61 | R |
| F106 | BRIGHTON | Yarrow | 1957—61 | R |
| F107 | ROTHESAY | Yarrow | 1956—60 | R |
| F108 | LONDONDERRY | White | 1956—60 | R |
| F113 | FALMOUTH | S. Hunter | 1957—61 | R |
| F115 | BERWICK | Har.Wolff | 1958—61 | R |
| F126 | PLYMOUTH | HMD.Dev. | 1958—61 | R |
| F129 | RHYL | HMD.Ports | 1958—60 | R |

SCARBOROUGH

# 15 Type 12 Anti-submarine frigates

First of the large type frigates built for a.s work. The first to be completed are known as the Whitbys, and the last nine as the Rothesays. This last group had improvements built into them after experience in service of the first 6. Most of them have been rebuilt and are now of quite different appearance than when first completed. A very successful type in service they are the forerunners of the excellent Leander frigates. BLACKPOOL at present unarmed after return from New Zealand Navy. Is being refitted as a trials ship.

M       tons Whitby 2150/2160
             Rothesay 2380/2800
D       112.8 x 12.5 x 5.3
Mch     ST 30000 hp 30k
C       235

| No. | 4.5 | 3" RP | 20 mm | Mast | SC. | 40 mm | Lim | Heli |
|---|---|---|---|---|---|---|---|---|
| F36 | 2 | 2 | | L | | 1 | 2 | N |
| F43 | 2 | 2 | | T | | | 1 | N |
| F63 | 2 | | | L | | | 2 | N |
| F65 | 2 | | | L | | 1 | 2 | N |
| F73 | | | | L | | 1 | | N |
| F77 | | | | | | | | |
| F101 | 2 | 2 | 2 | T | 1 | | 1 | Y |
| F103 | 2 | 2 | 2 | T | 1 | | 1 | Y |
| F106 | 2 | 2 | 2 | T | 1 | | 1 | Y |
| F107 | 2 | 2 | 2 | T | 1 | | 1 | Y |
| F108 | 2 | 2 | 2 | T | 1 | | 1 | Y |
| F113 | 2 | 2 | 2 | T | 1 | | 1 | Y |
| F115 | 2 | 2 | 2 | T | 1 | | 1 | Y |
| F126 | 2 | 2 | 2 | T | 1 | | 1 | Y |
| F129 | | | | | | | | |

| Number | Name | Builder | Date of Building |
|---|---|---|---|
| F14 | LEOPARD | HMD.Ports | 1953—58 |
| F27 | LYNX | Brown | 1953—57 |
| F34 | PUMA | Scotts | 1953—57 |
| F37 | JAGUAR | Denny | 1953—59 |
| F32 | SALISBURY | HMD.Dev. | 1952—57 |
| F59 | CHICHESTER | Fairfield | 1953—58 |
| F61 | LLANDAFF | Hawthorn | 1953—58 |
| F99 | LINCOLN | Fairfield | 1955—60 |

PUMA — Funnel in lattice foremast

LINCOLN — American style Mack 'stack' in
tower foremast

## LEOPARD Class

Designed as anti-craft frigates to work in conjunction with the WHITBYS and provide air cover and a surface offensive capability in a frigate group. Since completion have served world wide, they are likely to be withdrawn from service as the new frigates join the fleet.

```
M      2300/2520
D      100.6 x 12.2 x 4.9
Mch    Dsl 12400 bhp = 25k
C      235
```

## SALISBURY Class

This class was to provide long range air warning air direction for frigate groups. The large hull was required as the radar of the period was bulky and complex compared with modern systems.

```
M.     2170/2408 f.l.
D      100.6 x 40 x 4.7
Mch    Dsl 12400 bhp = 25k
C      237
```

|      | 4.5 | 40 mm | 20 mm | RP | SC | SQ |
|------|-----|-------|-------|----|----|----|
| F14  | 4   | 1     | 2     | 2  |    | 1  |
| F27  | 4   | 1     |       | 2  |    | 1  |
| F34  | 4   | 1     |       | 2  |    | 1  |
| F37  | 4   | 1     | 1     | 2  |    | 1  |
| F32  | 2   | 2     |       | 2  | 1  | 1  |
| F59  | 2   | 2     |       | 2  |    | 1  |
| F61  | 2   | 2     |       | 2  |    | 1  |
| F99  | 2   |       | 2     | 2  | 1  | 1  |

| Number | Name | Builders | Date of Building |
|---|---|---|---|
| F117 | ASHANTI | Yarrow | 1958—61 |
| F119 | ESKIMO | White | 1958—63 |
| F122 | GURKHA | Thornby | 1958—63 |
| F124 | ZULU | Stephen | 1960—64 |
| F125 | MOHAWK | Vickers | 1960—63 |
| F131 | NUBIAN | HMD.Ports | 1959—62 |
| F133 | TARTAR | HMD.Dev. | 1959—62 |
| F76 | MERMAID | Yarrow | 1965—73 |

MOHAWK

MERMAID — Only Royal Navy ship with
bowl-shaped radar

# TRIBAL Class

General purpose frigate designed to carry out a variety of roles. Since completion their main task has been to show the flag on foreign stations. They are the last of the colonial Aviso's of the days of the Empire. They are the first Royal Navy frigates built to carry a helicopter and the first to have steam and gas turbines for propulsion.

| | |
|---|---|
| M | 2300/2700 f.l. |
| D | 109.7 x 12.9 x 5.3 |
| Mch | ST and GT 20000 shp = 28k |
| C | 253 |

# MERMAID

Built for the Ghanaian Navy she was cancelled before completion. She was subsequently completed for the Royal Navy. A general purpose frigate used for the same sort of duties as the Tribals.

| | |
|---|---|
| M | 2300/2525 f.l. |
| D | 105 x 12 x 3 |
| Mch | Dsl 16000 bhp 25k |
| C | 227 |

| | 4.5 | 40 mm | 20 mm | RB | SC | LI | VDS |
|---|---|---|---|---|---|---|---|
| F177 | 2 | | 2 | 2 | 2 | 1 | Y |
| F119 | 2 | 2 | | | | 1 | N |
| F122 | 2 | | 2 | 2 | 2 | 1 | Y |
| F124 | 2 | | | 2 | 2 | 1 | N |
| F125 | 2 | | 2 | 2 | 2 | 1 | N |
| F131 | 2 | | 2 | 2 | 2 | 1 | N |
| F133 | 2 | | 2 | 2 | 2 | 1 | N |
| F76 | 2(4") 4 | | | | | 1 | N |

| Number | Name | Builder | Date of Building |
|---|---|---|---|
| F 48 | DUNDAS | White | 1952—56 |
| F 54 | HARDY | Yarrow | 1953—55 |
| F 78 | BLACKWOOD | Thorny | 1953—57 |
| F 80 | DUNCAN | Thorny | 1953—58 |
| F 84 | EXMOUTH | White | 1954—57 |
| F 85 | KEPPEL | Yarrow | 1953—56 |
| F 88 | MALCOLM | Yarrow | 1954—57 |
| F 94 | PALLISER | Stephen | 1955—57 |
| F 97 | RUSSELL | S. Hunter | 1953—57 |

# BLACKWOOD Class Type 14

During the cold war of the 1950s there was thought to be a need for a simple type of anti-submarine frigate, able to be built quickly in large numbers if required. The result of this thinking was the type 14 utility frigate. Although they carried a light gun armament they had for their time a powerful anti-sub capacity and a speed high enough to deal with the subs then in service. They have since been overtaken by advances in submarine design and three of the class have been scrapped and others laid up. All will be disposed of as the modern frigate enter service. In 1968 EXMOUTH was fitted with gas turbine and used as a test bed for this machinery now being fitted to all the modern construction.

| | |
|---|---|
| M | 1180/1456 f.l. |
| D | 94.5 x 10 x 4.7 |
| Mch | ST 15000 shp = 27.8k |
| | F84    GT 22500 hp = 28k |
| C | 140 |

### ARMAMENT OF ALL THAT REMAIN IN SERVICE

| 40mm | LI | RP |
|---|---|---|
| 2 | 2 | 1 |

EXMOUTH — Converted for gas turbine
propulsion 'test-bed'

DUNDAS — All class same appearance

# MINE WARFARE VESSELS

| Number | Name | Builder | Date of Building | Operations |
|---|---|---|---|---|
| M1103 | KILMOREY | Thornby | 1953 | MCM |
| M1109 | KILLIECRANKIE | White | 1953 | MCM |
| M1110 | BILDESTON | Doig | 1953 | MH |
| M1112 | BOULSTON | Richards | 1953 | MCM |
| M1113 | BRERETON | Richards | 1955 | MH |
| M1114 | BRINTON | C.W.G. | 1953 | MH |
| M1115 | BRONINGTON | C.W.G. | 1953 | MH |
| M1116 | WILTON | Vosper | 1973 | MCM |
| M1124 | ST. DAVID | Doig | 1953 | MCM |
| M1125 | CUXTON | Camper N | 1954 | MCM |
| M1130 | HIGHBURTON | Thornby | 1955 | MCM |
| M1133 | BOSSINGTON | Thornby | 1956 | MH |
| M1136 | CURZON | White | 1954 | MCM |
| M1140 | GAVINGTON | Doig | 1954 | MH |
| M1141 | GLASSERTON | Doig | 1954 | MCM |
| M1145 | DUFTON | Goole | 1955 | MCM |
| M1146 | VENTURER | Fleetlands | 1954 | MCM |
| M1147 | HUBBERSTON | Camper N | 1955 | MH |
| M1150 | INVERMORISTON | Dorset | 1955 | MCM |
| M1151 | INVESTON | Philip | 1955 | MH |
| M1153 | KEDLESTON | Pickersgill | 1954 | MH |
| M1154 | KELLINGTON | Pickersgill | 1955 | MH |
| M1157 | KIRKLISTON | Har.Wolff | 1954 | MH |

| M1158 | LALESTON | Har.Wolff | 1954 | DT |
| M1161 | LEVERTON | Har.Wolff | 1955 | MCM |
| M1164 | MADDISTON | Har.Wolff | 1956 | MCM |
| M1165 | MAXTON | Har.Wolff | 1956 | MH |
| M1166 | NURTON | Har.Wolff | 1957 | MH |
| M1167 | CLYDE | Har.Wolff | 1958 | MCM |
| M1173 | MERSEY | Camper N | 1958 | MCM |
| M1175 | QUAINTON | Richards | 1958 | MCM |
| M1180 | SHAVINGTON | White | 1955 | MCM |
| M1181 | SHERATON | White | 1956 | MH |
| M1182 | SHOULTON | Montrose | 1955 | MH |
| M1187 | UPTON | Thorny | 1956 | MCM |
| M1188 | WALKERTON | Thornby | 1957 | MH |
| M1192 | WILKESTON | C.W.G. | 1957 | MCM |
| M1194 | THAMES | Herd Mc. | 1958 | MCM |
| M1195 | WOTTON | Philip | 1956 | MCM |
| M1198 | ASHTON | White | 1957 | MCM |
| M1199 | BELTON | Doig | 1957 | MCM |
| M1200 | SOBERTON | Fleetlands | 1957 | MCM |
| M1204 | MONTROSE | Camper N | 1957 | MCM |
| M1205 | NORTHUMBRIA | Wivenhoe | 1959 | MCM |
| M1206 | FISKERTON | Doig | 1957 | MCM |
| M1208 | LEWISTON | Herd.Mc. | 1960 | MCM |
| M1209 | CHAWTON | Fleetlands | 1958 | MCM |
| M1216 | SOLENT | Thornby | 1958 | MCM |

CHAWTON — Fitted for fishery protection with searchlight aft and rubber boat alongside funnel

GLASSERTON — Typical Mine Countermeasure craft

BRINTON

# TON Class Mine countermeasures

Numerically the largest class of warship built for the Royal Navy postwar. Capable of dealing with all types of mine. Some of this class have been sold and are now serving with many other navies. Other navies have also built mine countermeasures vessels to the same basic design. A very versatile type they have been used as fishery protection vessels, and as patrol gunboats for anti-terrorist work in the Mediterranean and Far East. The designed armament of 1—40mm and 2—20mm has been retained by most of the class though some have had the 2—20mm removed while others mount 2—40mm. Some have been converted to Mine Hunters(MH) and have had the LL Magnetic sweep removed and extra stowage added for Gemini craft with davit to handle them. Those that have retained the LL are now classed as mine countermeasures (MCM). All have wooden hulls except M1116 WILTON, which is the Royal Navy's first plastic hulled warship.

```
M      360/425 f.l.
D      46 x 8 x 2.5
Mch    Dsl 3000 bhp= 15k
C      27(MCM)  36(MH)
```

| Number | Name | Builder | Date of Building | Operations |
|---|---|---|---|---|
| M2002 | AVELEY | White | 1953 | TT |
| M2010 | ISIS | Saunders | 1955 | TT |
| M2603 | ARLINGHAM | Camper N | 1953 | TRV |
| M2611 | BOTTISHAM | Ailsa | 1953 | RAF |
| M2614 | BUCKLESHAM | Ardrossan | 1954 | TRV |
| M2616 | CHELSHAM | Buckie | 1952 | RAF |
| M2621 | DITTISHAM | Fairlie | 1954 | TT |
| M2622 | DOWNHAM | White | 1956 | TRV |
| M2624 | ELSINGHAM | Ailsa | 1955 | |
| M2626 | EVERINGHAM | Philip | 1954 | TRV |
| M2628 | FLINTHAM | Boulson | 1955 | TT |
| M2630 | FRITHAM | Brooke | 1954 | TRV |

| M2635 | HAVERSHAM | McLean | 1955 | TRV |
| M2636 | LASHAM | Weatherhead | 1954 | TRV |
| M2716 | PAGHAM | Jones | 1956 | RNXS |
| M2717 | FORDHAM | Jones | 1957 | DGV |
| M2726 | SHIPHAM | Brooke | 1956 | RNXS |
| M2733 | THAKEHAM | Fairlie | 1958 | RNXS |
| M2735 | TONGHAM | Miller | 1956 | RNXS |
| M2737 | WARMINGHAM | Thorny | 1954 | DGV |
| M2781 | PORTISHAM | Dorset | 1956 | RNXS |
| M2783 | ODIHAM | Vosper | 1956 | RNXS |
| M2784 | PUTTENHAM | Thorny | 1957 | RNXS |
| M2785 | BIRDHAM | Taylor | 1956 | RNXS |
| M2790 | THATCHAM | Jones | 1958 | DGV |
| M2791 | SANDRINGHAM | McLean | 1957 | PAS |
| M2793 | THORNHAM | Taylor | 1957 | TT |

## HAM and LEY Class

Large class of inshore minesweepers built from experience
from operations in  WWII. The HAMs were minesweepers and
the LEYs minehunters. Their construction was prompted by
the cold war of the 1950s and as the situation thawed many
were laid up on completion without being commissioned.
After a fairly short period of active service many were laid up
or sold to other navies. Those that remain have been adapted
or converted for other roles as follows :-

|  |  |  |
|---|---|---|
| DGV | = | Degaussing Vessels |
| PAS | = | Port Auxiliary Service |
| RAF | = | Royal Air Force |
| RNXS | = | Royal Naval Aux. Ser. |
| TRV | = | Torpedo Recovery Vessels |
| TT | = | Training Tenders |

M    120/159 f.l. (LEYs 123/164 f.l.)
D    32 x 6.5 x 1.5
Mch    Dsl 1100 bhp = 14k (LEYs 700 bhp = 13k.)
C    8 to 20

# Off Shore Oil/Gas Rig Protection Vessels

Five of these ships are to be built, they will be ready for services by 1977. Displ will be approx. 900t. speed 16k. They will be armed with 40mm guns and probably a simple type of surface-to-surface missile. Until completion this task will be carried out by JURA and REWARD Q.V.

PORTISHAM — Fitted for minesweeping

WARMINGHAM — Converted for DGV

# COASTAL PATROL CRAFT

| Number | Name | Builder | Date of Building |
|---|---|---|---|
| P260 | KINGFISHER | Dunston | 1973— |
| P261 | CYGNET | Dunston | 1973— |
| P262 | PETREL | Dunston | 1973— |
| P263 | SANDPIPER | Dunston | 1973— |
| P271 | SCIMITAR | Vosper | 1969—70 |
| P174 | CUTLASS | Vosper | 1969—70 |
| P275 | SABRE | Vosper | 1970—71 |
| P276 | TENACITY | Vosper | 1968—69 |
| P1007 | BEACHAMPTON | Goole | 1952—54 |
| P1055 | MONCKTON | H & McKenzie | 1955—56 |
| P1089 | WASPERTON | Whites | 1955—56 |
| P1093 | WOLVERTON | Montrose | 1956—57 |
| P1096 | YARNTON | Pickersgill | 1956—57 |
|  | JURA |  |  |
|  | DOLWEN | Harris | 1962 |

TENACITY — Fitted for fishery protection

# KINGFISHER Class

Under construction, new type of coastal patrol craft.

# SCIMITAR Class

Built for training Royal Navy units to intercept and destroy possible enemy missile boats. No armament.

M       102 f.l.
D       31 x 8.5 x 1.5
Mch     GT and Dsl 40 k plus
C       12

# TENACITY

Built by Vospers as a private venture Fast Missile Boat. Taken over by the Royal Navy 1971. Now used for Fishery Protection.

M       165/220 f.l.
D       44 x 8 x 2
Mch     GT and Dsl 12750 bhp = 40 k
C       27

# BEACHAMPTON Class

Former TON class minesweepers with sweep gear removed and armed with 2—40mm. Re-classified as Patrol Gunboats and stationed in the Far East.
See TON class for details.

# JURA

Former Fishery Protection, Scottish Fisheries. Commissioned into Royal Navy 1975. Now Oil/Gas Rig Patrol Vessel. Armed with 1.40 mm.

# DOLWEN

Civilian stern trawler purchased by Royal Navy and commissioned in 1974.

# NUCLEAR SUBMARINES

| Number | Name | Builders | Date of Building |
|---|---|---|---|
| S101 | DREADNOUGHT | Vickers | 1959—63 |
| S104 | CHURCHILL | Vickers | 1967—70 |
| S105 | CONQUEROR | Cam.Laird | 1967—71 |
| S106 | COURAGEOUS | Vickers | 1970—71 |
| S102 | VALIANT | Vickers | 1962—66 |
| S103 | WARSPITE | Vickers | 1963—67 |
| S110 | SCEPTRE | Vickers | 1973 |
| S108 | SOVEREIGN | Vickers | 1970—74 |
| S111 | SPARTAN | Vickers | |
| S109 | SUPERB | Vickers | 1971— |
| S107 | SWIFTSURE | Vickers | 1969—73 |
| S26 | RENOWN | Cam.Laird | 1964—69 |
| S23 | REPULSE | Vickers | 1965—68 |
| S22 | RESOLUTION | Cam.Laird | 1964—67 |
| S27 | REVENGE | Vickers | 1965—69 |

Valiant and Swiftsure Classes

Dreadnought

# DREADNOUGHT

The Royal Navy's first Nuclear powered warship, designed to hunt and kill enemy submarines and armed with six 21" bow torpedo tubes.

M     3000/3500 f.l. 4000 sub.
D      81 x 9.8 x 7.9
Mch  Nuclear/ST 30k plus
C      88

# VALIANT and S Class

Nuclear patrol subs with unlimited range and endurance. Capable of hunting and killing enemy underwater and surface craft. Armed with six 21" bow torpedo tubes (S class five)

M     3500  4500 sub (S 3800/4800 sub)
D      86.9 x 10.1 x 8.2  (S 84 x 9.7 x 8.2)
Mch  Nuclear/ST 35k plus.
C      103 (S 97)

# RESOLUTION Class

These are the capital ships of today's navy. Nuclear powered and and armed with 16 Polaris missiles and six 21" torpedo tubes. The missiles have a range of 2500 miles.

M     7500/8400 sub.
D      129.5 x 10.1 x 9.1
Mch  Nuclear/ST 30k plus.
C      141

Resolution

# CONVENTIONAL SUBMARINES

| Number | Name | Builder | Date of Building |
|---|---|---|---|
| S09 | OBERON | HMD Chat. | 1957—61 |
| S17 | OCELOT | HMD Chat. | 1960—64 |
| S10 | ODIN | Cam.Laird | 1959—62 |
| S12 | OLYMPUS | Vickers | 1960—62 |
| S14 | ONSLAUGHT | HMD Chat. | 1959—62 |
| S21 | ONYX | Cam.Laird | 1964—67 |
| S19 | OPOSSUM | Cam.Laird | 1961—64 |
| S20 | OPPORTUNE | Scotts | 1962—64 |
| S16 | ORACLE | Cam.Laird | 1960—63 |
| S11 | ORPHEUS | Vickers | 1959—60 |
| S13 | OSIRIS | Vickers | 1962—64 |
| S15 | OTTER | Scotts | 1960—62 |
| S18 | OTUS | Scotts | 1961—63 |
| S06 | CACHALOT | Scotts | 1955—59 |
| S05 | FINWHALE | Cam.Laird | 1956—60 |
| S04 | GRAMPUS | Cam.Laird | 1955—58 |
| S03 | NARWHAL | Vickers | 1956—59 |
| S01 | PORPOISE | Vickers | 1954—58 |
| S02 | PORQUAL | Vickers | 1955—58 |
| S07 | SEALION | Cam.Laird | 1958—61 |
| S08 | WALRUS | Scotts | 1958—61 |

# OBERON Class    PORPOISE Class

Same dimensions but five tons heavier on standard displacement than the earlier PORPOISE Class., due to the improved anti-submarine equipment fitted. Conventional submarine propulsion, diesel on surface and electric submerged. All units have snort, they are the last conventional powers vessels to be built for the Royal Navy. Both classes are armed with eight 21" torpedo tubes, six bow and two stern. PORQUAL will be first of these vessels to be withdrawn from service, she is to be laid up within next 12 months.

```
M      1610/2405 f.l. 2410 sub
D      90 x 8.1 x 5.5
Mch    Dsl 3680 bhp 12k    Electric 6000 shp. 17k
C      OB 68  PO 71
```

Typical of both classes of diesel powered submarine

# SURVEY CRAFT

| Number | Name | Builder | Date of Building |
|---|---|---|---|
| | HECATE | Yarrow | 1964—65 |
| | HECLA | Yarrow | 1964—65 |
| | HERALD | Robb | 1972—74 |
| | HYDRA | Yarrow | 1964—66 |
| | BEAGLE | Brooke | 1966—68 |
| | BULLDOG | Brooke | 1966—68 |
| | FAWN | Brooke | 1966—68 |
| | FOX | Brooke | 1966—68 |
| | ECHO | S. Wnite | 1958 |
| | EGERIA | Weatherhead | 1959 |
| | ENTERPRISE | Blackmore | 1959 |
| | WATERWITCH<br>ex-POWDERHAM | White | 1959 |
| | WOODLARK<br>ex-YAXHAM | | 1958 |
| A171 | ENDURANCE | Kroger | 1957 |

# HECLA Class

Ships designed and built especially for survey work as opposed to earlier survey vessels which were converted warships or warship design. Equipped for ocean survey all ships carry one Wasp helicopter.

```
M      1915/2733 (HERALD 2945)
D      79.3 x 15 x 4.7
Mch    Dsl/Electric 2000 shp = 14k
C      118 to 125
```

# FAWN Class

Coastal survey vessels built for working in shallow waters. Able to operate world wide.

```
M      800/1088 f.l.
D      57 x 11 x 3.6
Mch    Dsl 2000 bhp = 15k
C      38
```

# ECHO Class

Inshore survey craft for working in confined coastal waters and harbours. Convertable to minehunters if required with mounting forward for one—40mm. As survey craft they are unarmed.

```
M      120/160 f.l.
D      32 x 6.5 x 1.5
Mch    Dsl 700 bhp = 14k
C      18 to 22
```

# WATERWITCH Class

Converted HAM Class inshore minesweepers. Used for inshore survey in home waters. Now replaced by the ECHO Class. For details see HAM Class.

# ENDURANCE

Ex merchant ship ANITA DAN purchased from the Danish Lauritzen lines. Commissioned for her first patrol in 1958. She was converted for a dual purpose ice patrol and surveyor ship operating in the Antarctic. Her hull is painted bright red to enable her to be easily spotted in the ice and snow of the Antarctic. Two Whirlwind helicopters are carried.

```
M      3600
D      92 x 14 x 5.5
Mch    Dsl 3220 ihp = 14.5k
C      119 to 130
```

# SUPPORT & EXPERIMENTAL CRAFT

| Number | Name | Builder | Date of Building |
|---|---|---|---|
| A108 | TRIUMPH | Hawthorn | 1943—46 |
| A185 | MAIDSTONE | J.Brown | 1936—38 |
| A187 | DEFIANCE | J.Brown | 1926—38 |
| A231 | RECLAIM | Simons | 1946—48 |
| A354 | WHITEHEAD | Scotts | 1969—71 |
| A387 | GIRDLENESS | Burrard | 1944—45 |
| | CRYSTAL | HMD Dev | 1970—72 |
| | ICEWHALE | | |
| | SAREPTA | Norddeutsche | 1922 |
| | WHIMBREL | | |
| | THOMAS GRANT | Hill | 1953 |
| | TORRENT | S.Hunter | 1971 |
| | TORRID | S.Hunter | 1972 |
| N13 | MINER 111 | Philip | 1940 |
| N21 | ABDIEL | Thornycr | 1967 |
| | BRITANNIC | Philip | 1941 |
| | STEADY | Philip | 1944 |
| D43 | MATAPAN | Clydebank | 1944—47 |

# TRIUMPH

Ex aircraft carrier converted into heavy repair ship. Commissioned as such in 1965.

# MAIDSTONE    DEFIANCE

Submarine depot ship, refitted in 1962 to handle nuclear subs. At present in Northern Ireland as Headquarters/Accommodation ship. Sister ship FORTH renamed DEFIANCE and is now a harbour training ship.

# RECLAIM

Deep diving and submarine rescue ship.

# WHITEHEAD

Experimental trials vessel for torpedoes and associated equipment.

# GIRDLENESS

Formerly trials vessel for Sea Slug missiles, now in use as accommodation ship.

# CRYSTAL, ICEWHALE, SARPETA, WHIMBREL, THOMAS GRANT.

All experimental and trials vessels for underwater weapons.

# TORRENT, TORRID

Torpedo recovery vessels attached to submarine squadrons.

TORRID — Stern gate for torpedo recovery

# MINER 111, ABDIEL, BRITANNIC, STEADY

ABDIEL mine counter measures support ship, other three minelayers.

## MATAPAN

Former Battle Class Destroyer, converted for use as a sonar trials ship at Portsmouth in 1971—72.

| Name | Ton | Dim. | Mch. |
|---|---|---|---|
| TRIUMPH | 17000 fl | 213 x 24.4 x 7.2 | Steam Turbine 40000 shp=24k |
| MAIDSTONE DEFIANCE | 13000 fl 13000 fl | 161.8 x 22.3 x 6.5 | Steam Turbine 7000 shp=16k |
| RECLAIM | 1800 fl | 66 x 11.5 x 4.5 | Steam Recip. 1500 ihp=12k |
| WHITEHEAD | 3040 fl | 97 x 14.6 x | Diesel 3400 bhp=15½k |
| GIRDLENESS | 10200 fl | 134 x 6 x 17 | Steam Recip. 2500 ihp=10k |
| CRYSTAL | 3040 | 125 x 17 x 1.5 | Dumb |
| ICEWHALE | 350 fl | 36.5 x 7.3 x 2.7 | Diesel 9k |
| SARAPETA | 465 | 47 x 8 x 3.6 | Diesel 250bhp=9k |
| WHIMBREL | 350 fl | 57 x 9 x 1.3 | Diesel 920bhp=10k |
| THOMOGRANT | 461 fl | 34.4 x 7.8 x 2.7 | Diesel 500bhp=10k |
| TORRENT TORRID | | | Diesel |
| MINER 111 BRITANNIC STEADY | 355 fl | 33.5 x 7.9 x 2.4 | Diesel 360bhp=10k |
| ABDIEL | 1500 fl | 80 x 11.5 x 3 | Diesel 2690 bhp=16k |
| MATAPAN | | 115.5 x 12.3 x 5.5 | Steam Turbine 50000 shp=30k |

RECLAIM

BRITANNIC — Note wooden wheelhouse

MATAPAN — High hull, no armament

# FLEET OILERS

| Number | Name | Builder | Date of Building |
|---|---|---|---|
| A75 | TIDESPRING | Hawthorn | 1961—63 |
| A76 | TIDEPOOL | Hawthorn | 1961—63 |
| A96 | TIDEREACH | S.Hunter | 1953—55 |
| A97 | TIDEFLOW | Thompson | 1953—55 |
| A98 | TIDESURGE | Laing | 1953—55 |
| A122 | OLWEN | Hawthorn | 1963—65 |
| A123 | OLNA | Hawthorn | 1963—66 |
| A124 | OLMEDA | S.Hunter | 1963—65 |
| A268 | GREY ROVER | S.Hunter | 1968—70 |
| A269 | GREEN ROVER | S.Hunter | 1968—69 |
| A270 | BLUE ROVER | S.Hunter | 1968—70 |
| A271 | GOLD ROVER | S.Hunter | 1972— |
| A272 | BLACK ROVER | S. Hunter | 1972— |

TIDEPOOL — Helicopter hanger alongside funnel

# TIDE Class

First of the fleet replenishment ships designed to refuel
and store warships under weigh. As well as 13000 tons of
fuel oil they also carry dry stores of all types. A75 and 76 are
fitted to carry a helicopter.

M      9040/25940 f.l. (A75 76 8531/25931 f.l.)
D      179 x 21 x 9.7
Mch    ST 15000 shp = 17k.
C      115

# OL Class

Larger and faster ships embodying in their design all
the lessons learnt from operations with the earlier TIDE Class.
Three helicopters can be carried.

M      10890/33240 f.l.
D      197 x 25.6 x 10
Mch    ST 26500 shp = 21k
C      87

# ROVER Class

A smaller type of replenishment ship built to supply the
smaller frigate types now in service. When on detachment
with an escort group can keep them supplied with fuel oil,
aviation fuel, fresh water, general stores and refrigerated stores.
Capable of replenishing under weigh by normal methods or
by helicopter, which can also be used to supply ground
forces.

M      11522 f.l.
D      140 x 19 x 7.3
Mch    Dsl 16000 bhp = 19k
C      42

GREY ROVER

# BULK OIL VESSELS

| Number | Name | Builder | Date of Building |
|---|---|---|---|
| A77 | PEARLEAF | Blythswood | 1960 |
| A80 | ORANGELEAF | Furness | 1955 |
| A81 | BRAMBLELEAF | Furness | 1953 |
| A82 | CHERRYLEAF | Laing | 1963 |
| A219 | DEWDALE | H.Wolff | 1965 |
| A221 | DERWENTDALE | Hitachi | 1964 |
| A261 | EDDYFIRTH | Lobnitz | 1954 |
| | OILBIRD | Appledore | 1969 |
| | OILFIELD | Appledore | 1969 |
| | OILMAN | Appledore | 1969 |
| | OILPRESS | Appledore | 1968 |
| | OILSTONE | Appledore | 1968 |
| | OILWELL | Appledore | 1969 |

ORANGELEAF

# LEAF and DALE Class

Merchant tankers chartered by the Royal Navy for the world wide transportation of fuel oil. All have a limited capability for refueling ships at sea.

|      | Ton          | Dim             | Mch                      | Former Name            |
| ---- | ------------ | --------------- | ------------------------ | ---------------------- |
| A77  | 24900 fl.    | 173 x 21 x 9    | Deisel 8800 bhp 15k      |                        |
| A80  | 17475dw      | 169 x 21 x 9    | Deisel 6800 bhp=15k      | SOUTHERN SATELLITE     |
| A81  | 17690dw      | 169 x 21 x 9    | Deisel 6800 bhp=14k      | LONDON LOYALTY         |
| A82  | 18560dw      | 165 x 21 x 9    | Deisel                   | OVERSEAS ADVENTURER    |
| A219 | 63588dw C 56 | 235 x 32 x 12   | Deisel 17000 bhp=15k     | EDENFIELD              |
| A221 | 72550dw C 51 | 243 x 35 x 12   | Deisel 20700 bhp=15.5k   | HALCYON BREEZE         |

# EDDYFIRTH

Last of a class of eight coastal tankers

| | |
| --- | --- |
| M   | 1960/4160 f.l. |
| D   | 87 x 13 x 5 |
| Mch | T.E. 1750 ihp = 12k |

# OILBIRD

New class of small tanker for work in naval harbours can undertake short coastal voyages.

| | |
| --- | --- |
| M   | 250dw |
| D   | 41.5 x 7 x 2.4 |
| Mch | Dsl 405 bhp = 10k |
| C   | 11 |

# FLEET REPLENISHMENT VESSELS

| Number | Name | Builder | Date of Building |
|---|---|---|---|
| A84 | RELIANT | Laing | 1955 |
| A280 | RESURGENT | Scotts | 1951 |
| A329 | RETAINER | Scotts | 1950 |
| A134 | RAME HEAD | Pacific | 1945 |
| A191 | BERRY HEAD | Burrard | 1945 |
| A339 | LYNESS | S.Hunter | 1966 |
| A344 | STROMNESS | S.Hunter | 1967 |
| A345 | TARBATNESS | S.Hunter | 1967 |
| A385 | FORT GRANGE | Scott | 1975 |
| A386 | FORT AUSTIN | Scott | 1975 |
| A480 | RESOURCE | Scott | 1967 |
| A486 | REGENT | H.Wolff | 1967 |
| A404 | BACCHUS | Robb | 1962 |
| A406 | HEBE | Robb | 1962 |
| A241 | ROBERT MIDDLETON | Grangemouth | 1938 |
|  | KINTERBURY | Philip | 1943 |
|  | THROSK | Philip | 1944 |
|  | RNAL 54 | Camper Nicholsons | 195? |
|  | BRITANNIA | J.Brown | 1952—54 |

## RELIANT

Former merchant ship purchased and converted in 1958 as air stores support ship. She is equipped to transfer aircraft spares at sea to carriers.

# RESURGENT    RETAINER

Both former merchant ships taken over in 1951 (A280) and 1952. Both vessels during the course of several refits have been fitted to transport naval stores of all types, and to transfer them at sea if required.

## LYNESS Class

Three modern ships with latest equipment for the carriage and transfer at sea of all type of naval and victualling stores. All are able to operate helicopters for the transfer of cargo from landing pad aft.

## FORT Class

Two fleet replenishment ships under construction.

## RESOURCE Class

Two large vessels designed to replenish warships at sea with ammunition and explosives in addition to normal stores and food. One helicopter is carried for vertical transfer.

## BACCHUS Class

Cargo carriers, built as merchant ships and taken over by the Royal Navy on completion.

RELIANT — Originally passenger ship.
Helicopter pad aft

## HEAD Class

War built standard type store ships, two of a class of
twenty three. These two were converted while under
construction to serve as maintenance ships. They are now rated
as escort maintenance ships. RAME HEAD is at present in
Northern Ireland as accommodation ship. BERRY HEAD is due
for disposal later this year.

## ROBERT MIDDLETON

General cargo coasters

## RNAL 54

One of a group of powered lighters built in the 1950s
to transport aircraft as deck cargo from ship to shore. This
one was in service up to 1972 there may be others laid
up at naval ports.

## KINTERBURY Class

Naval armament carriers

## BRITANNIA

Royal Yatch

|  | Ton | Dim | Mch | Former Name |
|---|---|---|---|---|
| A84 | 9290dw C 110 | 142 x 18 x 7.9 | Diesel 8350bhp=18k | SOMERSBY |
| A280 A329 | 7500dw | 145 x 18.8 x 8.8 | Diesel 6500bhp=15k | CHANGCHOW CHUNGKING |
| A134 A191 A339 A344 A345 A385 A386 | 22170fl C 425 7782dw C 184 | 134.6 x 17.5 x 6.9 159 x 21.9 x 7.8 | TE 2500ihp=10k Diesel 11520bhp=17k |  |
| A480 A486 | 19000fl C 182 | 195 x 23 x 7.9 | ST 20000shp=20k |  |
| A404 A406 | 5218dw C 57 | 115 x 16.7 x 6.7 | Diesel 5500bhp=15k |  |
| A241 | 1900fl C 17 | 67.6 x 10 x 4 | Diesel 960bhp=10.5k |  |
| KINT. THRO. | 1770fl | 61 x 10 x 3.9 | TE 900ihp=11k |  |
| BRIT. | 4961fl | 125 x 16.7 x 5 | ST 12000shp=22k |  |

**RAME HEAD — 2 large cranes**

**LYNESS**

**WATERSPOUT — No funnel**

# WATER CARRIERS

| Number | Name | Builders | Date of Building |
|---|---|---|---|
| | WATERCOURSE | Holmes | 1973— |
| | WATERFOWL | Holmes | 1973—74 |
| | WATERFALL | Drypool | 1965—66 |
| | WATERSHED | Drypool | 1966—67 |
| | WATERSIDE | Drypool | 1967—68 |
| | WATERSPOUT | Hepworth | 1966—67 |
| | SPABROOK | Philip | 1944 |
| | SPABURN | Philip | 1946 |
| | SPALAKE | Hill | 1946 |
| | SPAPOOL | Hill | 1946 |
| | FRESHBURN | Lytham | 1943 |
| | FRESHENER | Lytham | 1942 |
| | FRESHLAKE | Lytham | 1942 |
| | FRESHMERE | Lytham | 1942 |
| | FRESHPOND | Lytham | 1945 |
| | FRESHPOOL | Lytham | 1943 |
| | FRESHSPRING | Lytham | 1946 |

## WATER—SPA—FRESH Class

All fresh water tankers based at naval ports but capable of operating in coastal waters.

| | | | |
|---|---|---|---|
| WATER | 285gt. | 40 x 7 x 2.4 | Dsl 1100bhp=11k |
| SPA | 630dw | 52 x 9 x 3.6 | TE 675ihp=9k |
| FRESH | Displ. 594 | 38 x 7.6 x 3 | TE 450ihp=9½k |

# TUGS

| Number | Name | Builder | Date of Building |
|---|---|---|---|
|  | ROBUST | Holmes | 1970—74 |
|  | ROLLICKER | Holmes | 1970—73 |
|  | ROYSTERER | Holmes | 1970—72 |
| A89 | ADVICE | Inglis | 1959 |
| A90 | ACCORD | Inglis | 1958 |
|  | AGILE | Goole | 1959 |
|  | CONFIANCE | Inglis | 1956 |
|  | CONFIDENT | Inglis | 1956 |
|  | SAMSON | Hall | 1954 |
|  | SEA GIANT | Hall | 1955 |
|  | SUPERMAN | Hall | 1956 |
|  | DEXTEROUS | Yarrow | 1957 |
|  | DIRECTOR | Yarrow | 1957 |
|  | FAITHFUL | Yarrow | 1958 |
|  | FAVOURITE | Ferguson | 1959 |
|  | FORCEFUL | Yarrow | 1958 |
|  | GRINDER | Simons | 1959 |
|  | GRIPER | Simons | 1958 |
| A95 | TYPHOON | Robb | 1959 |
| A111 | CYCLONE | Robb | 1943 |
| A264 | REWARD | Robb | 1945 |
| A236 | WAKEFUL |  |  |
| A223 | NIMBLE | Russell | 1942 |

# ROBUST Class

Largest and most powerful tugs ever built for the Royal
Navy. Duties are long distance towing and salvage.

M     1630 f.l.
D     54 x 11 x 6.5
Mch  Dsl 4500 bhp = 15k
C     41 with salvage crew

# CONFIANCE Class

Large modern tugs, used for docking large vessels. Also
capable of deep sea towing and salvage.

M     760 f.l.
D     47 x 10.6 x 3
Mch  Dsl 1800 bhp = 13k
C     42 with salvage crew

# SAMSON CLASS

Large tugs with duties much the same as CONFIANCE Class.

M     1200 f.l.
D     54.8 x 11 x 4.2
Mch  TE 3000 ihp = 15k

AGILE — Purpose built Naval tug

# DEXTEROUS Class

The Royal Navy's last paddle tugs, built for handling large ships, especially aircraft carriers in confined waters. All have low superstructure and folding mast to enable them to get alongside carriers under the overhang of the flight deck.

```
M      710 f.l.
D      47.8 x 18 x 3
Mch    Dsl Electric 1600 shp = 13k
C      21
```

# TYPHOON Class

Medium tugs mainly employed on short sea towing work. It has recently been stated that REWARD of this class is to be armed with 40mm guns and employed as oil and gas rig protection vessel.

```
M      1630 f.l.
D      63 x 12 x 5
Mch    Dsl 4000 bhp = 16k
C      42
```

# WAKEFUL

Civilian tug recently purchased for naval service.

# NIMBLE

Last tug of a Class of 4 built World War II.

FORCEFUL — Twin funnelled modern power tug

ROYSTERER

DALMATIAN

| Number | Name | Builder | Date of Building |
|---|---|---|---|
| | AIREDALE | Scarr | 1962 |
| | ALSATIAN | Scarr | 1962 |
| | BASSET | Dunston | 1963 |
| | BOXER | Dunston | 1964 |
| | CAIRN | Doig | 1965 |
| | COLLIE | Rowhedge | 1964 |
| | CORGI | Rowhedge | 1964 |
| | DALMATIAN | Doig | 1965 |
| | DEERHOUND | Appledore | 1965 |
| | ELKHOUND | Appledore | 1966 |
| | HUSKY | Appledore | 1969 |
| | LABRADOR | Appledore | 1966 |
| | MASTIFF | Appledore | 1967 |
| | POINTER | Appledore | 1967 |
| | SALUKI | Appledore | 1969 |
| | SEALYHAM | Appledore | 1967 |
| | SETTER | Appledore | 1969 |
| | SHEEPDOG | Appledore | 1970 |
| | SPANIEL | Appledore | 1967 |

| AGATHA | Harris | 1961 |
| AGNES | Harris | 1961 |
| ALICE | Harris | 1961 |
| AUDREY | Harris | 1961 |
| BARBARA | Dunston | 1963 |
| BETTY | Dunston | |
| BRENDA | Dunston | 1963 |
| BRIDGET | Dunston | |

ALICE

FIONA

| CELIA | Pimblott | 1966 |
| CHARLOTTE | Pimblott | 1966 |
| CHRISTINE | | |
| CLARE | | |
| DAISY | Dunston | 1968 |
| DAPHNE | Dunston | 1969 |
| DORIS | Dunston | 1969 |
| DOROTHY | Dunston | 1969 |
| EDITH | Dunston | 1969 |
| FELICITY | Dunston | 1968 |
| FIONA | Hancock | 1973 |
| GEORGINA | Pembroke | 1973 |
| GWENDOLINE | Pembroke | 1973 |
| HELEN | Pembroke | 1973 |
| IRENE | Dunston | 1972 |
| ISABEL | Dunston | 1972 |
| JOAN | Dunston | 1973 |
| JOYCE | Dunston | 1973 |
| KATHLEEN | Dunston | 1973 |
| KITTY | Dunston | 1973 |
| LESLEY | Dunston | 1974 |
| LILLIAN | Dunston | 1973 |
| LILAH | Dunston | 1973 |
| MAY | Dunston | 1973 |
| MARY | Dunston | 1973 |
| MYRTLE | Dunston | 1973 |
| NANCY | Dunston | 1973 |
| NORAH | Dunston | 1973 |

# DOG Class

Medium harbour berthing tugs, built to replace the large number of war built tugs of this type. Two thin engine uptakes instead of the traditional funnel give a clear unobstructed view aft.

M     152 g.
D     28.6 x 7.4 x 3.6
Mch   Dsl 1320 bhp = 12k

# GIRL Class

Small harbour berthing tugs again built to replace the once numerous TID type. There are four groups, 1st. AGATHA to BRIDGET have no funnel. 2nd. CELIA to EDITH (Modified Girl Class) have twin uptakes as the Dog Class. 3rd. FELICITY to HELEN (Large Water Tractor) Large superstructure with prominent funnel amidships. 4th. IRENE to NORAH (Small Water Tractor) Small wheelhouse amidships with small funnel joined to the rear.

M     40g (2nd 38g) (3rd 80g)
D     18 x 5 x 2.4 (2nd 20 x 6 x 2.7) (3rd 24 x 6.4 x 3)
Mch   1st and 2nd Dsl 495 bhp = 10k
      (3rd Dsl 600 bhp = 10k)
      (4th Dsl 600 bhp = 10k)

The 3rd and 4th groups are fitted with Voith-Schneider propellors forward and aft and are very manoeuverable.

FIONA & IRENE — Girl Class tugs

| Number | Name | Builder | Date of Building |
|---|---|---|---|
| | HANDMAID | Hall | 1940 |
| | IMPETUS | Hall | 1940 |
| | EMINENT | | 1946 |
| | EMPIRE NETTA | Fleming | 1945 |
| | EMPIRE ROSA | Blyth | 1946 |
| | FRISKY | Ferguson | 1946 |
| | RESOLVE | Fleming | 1946 |
| | BEHEST | Goole | 1944 |
| | EMPIRE ACE | Cochrane | 1942 |
| | EMPIRE DEMON | Brown | 1943 |
| | VAGRANT | Scott | 1943 |
| | WEASEL | Scott | 1945 |
| | DRIVER | Hall | 1942 |
| | EMPIRE FRED | Hall | 1943 |
| | FIDGET | Hall | 1944 |
| | PROMPT | Hall | 1943 |
| | SECURITY | Hall | 1946 |
| | TAMPEON | Yarwood | 1938 |
| | TRUNNION | Yarwood | 1938 |
| | FOREMOST | | 1938 |

Medium and small habour berthing tugs of wartime construction now being replaced by the Dog and Girl class. Some of these are laid up and may have already been sold.

# TANK CLEANING & MOORING VESSELS

| Number | Name | Builder | Date of Building |
|---|---|---|---|
|  | BERN | C.W.G. | 1942 |
|  | CALDY | Lewis | 1944 |
|  | COLL | Ardrossan | 1942 |
|  | GRAEMSAY | Ardrossan | 1943 |
|  | LUNDY | C.W.G. | 1943 |
|  | SKOMER | Lewis | 1943 |
|  | SWITHA | Inglis | 1942 |
|  | GARGANEY | Brooke | 1966 |
|  | GOLDENEYE | Brooke | 1966 |
|  | GOOSANDER | Robb | 1974 |
|  | MANDARIN | C.Laird | 1964 |
|  | PINTAIL | C.Laird | 1964 |
|  | POCHARD | Robb | 1974 |
|  | LAYBURN | Simons | 1960 |
|  | LAYMOOR | Simons | 1960 |
|  | DISPENSER | Smith | 1943 |
|  | KINBRACE | Hall | 1945 |
|  | KINGARTH | Hall | 1944 |
|  | KINLOSS | Hall | 1945 |
|  | UPLIFTER | Smith | 1944 |
|  | BARFOOT | Lewis | 1943 |
|  | BARMOND | Simons | 1943 |

# BERN Class

Last seven out of a total of one hundred and forty five
ISLES class trawlers built for the Royal Navy during the
last war. One other serves with the Royal Corps of Transport
see MULL. All the others have been sold to other navies or to
commercial owners. Fourteen were war losses. All of the
seven remaining were converted to tank cleaning vessels
in the early 1950s.

| | |
|---|---|
| M | 770 f.l. |
| D | 49 x 8.4 x 4.2 |
| Mch | TE 850 ihp = 12k |

# GARGENY LAYBURN DISPENSER BARFOOT

All of these ships are mooring, salvage and boom defence
vessels.

GARGENY

| | |
|---|---|
| Ton | 950 |
| D | 51 x 10.9 x 3 |
| Mch | Dsl 550 bhp = 10k |

LAYBURN

| | |
|---|---|
| Ton | 1050 f.l. |
| D | 59 x 10 x 3.4 |
| Mch | TE 1300 ihp = 10k |

DISPENSER

| | |
|---|---|
| Ton | 1050 f.l. |
| D | 54 x 10.6 x 3.6 |
| Mch | Dsl 630 bhp = 9k |
| | TE 600 ihp = 9k |

BARFOOT

| | |
|---|---|
| Ton | 1000 f.l. |
| D. | 55 x 7 x 3.3 |
| Mch | TE 850 ihp = 9k |

GOLDENEYE — Modern boom defence vessel

| Number | Name | Builder | Date of Building |
|---|---|---|---|
| | SALVEDA | Laird | 1943 |
| | SALVALOUR | Goole | 1945 |
| | SEA SALVOUR | Goole | 1943 |
| | BULLFINCH | S.Hunter | 1941 |
| | ST. MARGARETS | S.Hunter | 1944 |

RNAL 54

# SALVEDA and two SALVALOUR

Ocean salvage vessels, wartime construction at present laid up.


# BULLFINCH Class

Both cable ships


SALVEDA
Ton    1360 f.1
D       60 x 10 x 3.6
Mch    TE 1200 ihp = 12k

SALVALOUR
Ton    17000 f.1.
D       66 x 1.2 x 3.9
Mch    ST. TE 1500 ihp = 12k

BULLFINCH
Ton    2500 f.1
D       76 x 10.9 x 4.8
Mch    ST TE 1250 ihp = 12k

# FLEET TENDERS

| Number | Name | Builder | Date of Building |
|---|---|---|---|
| | ABERDOVY | Pimblott | 1963 |
| | ABINGER | Pimblott | 1964 |
| | ALNESS | Pimblott | 1964 |
| | ALNMOUTH | Pimblott | 1964 |
| | APPLEBY | Pimblott | 1965 |
| | ASHCOTT | Pimblott | 1965 |
| | BEAULIEU | Doig | 1963 |
| | BEDDGLERT | Doig | 1963 |
| | BEMBRIDGE | Doig | 1964 |
| | BIBURY | Doig | 1964 |
| | BLAKENEY | Doig | 1964 |
| | BRODICK | Doig | 1964 |
| | CARTMEL | Pimblott | 1968 |
| | CAWSAND | Pimblott | 1968 |
| | CRICCIETH | Pimblott | 1969 |
| | CRICKLADE | Holmes | 1969 |
| | CROMARTY | Lewis | 1970 |
| | DATCHET | Vosper | |
| | DENMEAD | Holmes | 1970 |
| | DORNOCH | Lewis | 1970 |
| | DUNSTER | Dunston | 1970 |
| | ELKSTONE | Cook | 1969 |
| | ELSING | Cook | 1970 |
| | EPWORTH | Cook | 1969 |

| ETTRICK | Cook | 1970 |
| FELSTED | Dunston | 1969 |
| FINTRY | Lewis | 1969 |
| FOTHERBY | Dunston | 1970 |
| FROXFIELD | Dunston | 1970 |
| FULBECK | Holmes | 1969 |
| GLENCOVE | Pimblott | 1969 |
| GRASMERE | Lewis | 1969 |
| HAMBLEDON | Dunston | 1972 |
| HARLECH | Dunston | 1972 |
| HEADCORN | Dunston | 1972 |
| HEVER | Dunston | 1972 |
| HOLMWOOD | Dunston | 1973 |
| HORNING | Dunston | 1973 |
| IXWORTH | Gregson | 1974 |
| LAMLASH | Dunston | 1974 |
| LECHLADE | Dunston | 1973 |
| LLANDOVERY | Dunston | 1973 |
| LOYAL CHANCELOR | Dunston | 1972 |

| Number | Name | Builder | Date of Building |
| --- | --- | --- | --- |
|  | BEE | Holmes | 1970 |
|  | CICALA | Holmes | 1970 |
|  | COCKCHAFER | Dunston | 1973 |
|  | CRICKET | Holmes | 1970 |
|  | GNAT | Holmes | 1970 |
|  | LADYBIRD | Holmes | 1971 |
|  | SCARAB | Holmes | 1971 |
| A | LOYAL PROCTOR | Dunston | 1973 |
| A220 | LOYAL MODERATOR | Dunston | 1973 |
| A308 | ILCHESTER | Gregson | 1974 |
| A309 | INSTOW | Gregson | 1974 |
| A310 | INVERGORDON | Gregson | 1974 |
| A311 | IRONBRIDGE | Gregson | 1974 |
| A382 | LOYAL FACTOR | Holmes | 1970 |
| A389 | CLOVELLY | Pimblott | 1970 |
| A510 | LOYAL GOVERNOR | Pimblott | 1970 |

APPLEBY — Tender (note lowered mast)

# ABERDOVY CARTMEL BEE

To replace the wooden MFVs built in large numbers during and just after the last war it was decided to order sixty fleet tenders. These are of steel construction as opposed to the wooden MFVs and are designed to carry out a variety of duties. The first group ABERDOVY have low upperworks so that they could get alongside under the  overhang of aircraft carriers. They can carry 200 standing passengers or 25 tons of cargo.

The second group CARTMEL have higher upperworks and greater beam. There are three types within this group, A. Cargo only. B.Passengers or cargo and C. With a crew of 12 fitted as training tenders. In time of war they could possibly be armed for harbour patrol.

The third group BEE are the largest and big enough for coastal and short sea voyages. They are again in three versions A. General cargo with two cranes. B. Cargo or armaments with one two ton crane. C. With a 3 ton crane and capable of lifting 10 ton over the bows as a mooring vessel.

ABERDOVY
Ton    117 f.l.
D      24 x 5.4 x 2.4
Mch    Dsl 225 bhp = 10½k

CARTMEL
Ton    143 f.l.
D      24 x 6.4 x 3
Mch    Dsl 320 bhp = 10½k

BEE
Ton    450 f.l.
D      33.8 x 8.5 x 3.3
Mch    Dsl 660 bhp = 10½k

HORNING

# ROYAL CORPS OF TRANSPORT

| Number | Name | Builder | Date of Building |
|---|---|---|---|
| RPL01 | AVON | | 1966 |
| RPL02 | BUDE | | 1966 |
| RPL03 | CLYDE | | 1966 |
| RPL04 | DART | | 1966 |
| RPL05 | EDEN | | 1966 |
| RPL06 | FORTH | | 1966 |
| RPL07 | GLEN | McLean | 1966 |
| RPL08 | HAMBLE | McLean | 1966 |
| RPL10 | KENNET | McLean | 1966 |
| RPL11 | LODDON | McLean | 1966 |
| RPL12 | MEDWAY | McLean | 1966 |
| WB03 | BREAM | | |
| WB04 | BARBEL | | |
| WB05 | ROACH | | |
| WB06 | PERCH | | |
| WB07 | PIKE | | |
| | MARTIN | | |
| | NEWMAN BLOGGS | | |
| | OLIVER TWIST | | |
| | SKUA | | |
| | SMIKE | | |
| | YARMOUTH NAVIGATOR | | |
| | YARMOUTH SEAMAN | | |
| | MULL | C.W.G. | 1941 |

# AVON

These are all manned and operated by the Army. They have accommodation aft and are able to make short coastal voyages. Of similar size to the Naval LCM they are diesel powered

# WB03 BREAM

Harbour work boats, also army manned.

# MARTIN

All of the large MFV type. Army manned general duties include personnel transport, target ranging, navigational training. The hulls are painted dark blue with white upper works.

# MULL

Ex. Isles class trawler, at present laid up.

ROACH — Army general purpose launch

# TRAINING & TARGET VESSELS

| Number | Name | Builder | Date of Building |
|---|---|---|---|
| D35 | DIAMOND | Clydebank | 1949—52 |
| D68 | BARROSA | Clydebank | 1943—47 |
| D01 | CAPRICE | Yarrow | 1942—44 |
| D73 | CAVALIER | S.White | 1943—44 |
| F53 | UNDAUNTED | C.Laird | 1942—44 |
| F138 | RAPID | C.Laird | 1941—43 |
| F187 | WHIRLWIND | Hawthorn | 1943—44 |
| F197 | GRENVILLE | S.Hunter | 1941—43 |
| F41 | VOLAGE | S.White | 1942—44 |

## DIAMOND to GRENVILLE

All these ships are laid up or in use as training or target vessels.

DIAMOND ex Daring Class destroyer now moored at Portsmouth and attached to HMS SULTAN for training.

D01, D68, D73, F41, F138 and F197 are all laid up awaiting disposal.

F53 and F187 are in use as target ships.

AVON — RPL-01

YARMOUTH NAVIGATOR

WHIRLWIND — As rigged for target practice

# ABBREVIATIONS

| | | |
|---|---|---|
| BHP | = | Brake Horse Power |
| C | = | Complement |
| D | = | Dimensions |
| Dsl | = | Diesel |
| DT | = | Diving Tender |
| DW | = | Deadweight |
| GT | = | Gas Turbine |
| gt | = | Gross Tonnage |
| Ex | = | Exocet |
| Heli | = | Helicopter |
| IHP | = | Initial Horse Power |
| IK | = | Ikara |
| K | = | Knots |
| L | = | Lattice Mast |
| Lim | = | Limbo |
| M | = | Measurement |
| Mch | = | Machinery |
| MCM | = | Mine Countermeasures |
| MH | = | Mine Hunter |
| N | = | No |
| Nu | = | Nuclear |
| P | = | Planned |
| RP | = | Rocket Projectors |
| SC | = | Sea Cat |
| SD | = | Sea Dart |
| SHP | = | Shaft Horse Power |
| ST | = | Steam Turbine |
| Sq | = | Squid |
| SS | = | Sea Slug |
| SW | = | Sea Wolf |
| T | = | Tower Mast |
| TE | = | Triple Expansion Steam |
| VDS | = | Variable Depth Sonar |
| Y | = | Yes |